What Do Authors and Illustrators Do?

by Eileen Christelow

HOUGHTON MIFFLIN HARCOURT

Boston New York

With love, to D R T H Y C who just finished writing a book about two giants.

This book is for Leonard and his two pals.

What Do Authors Do? first published in 1995 by Clarion Books and *What Do Illustrators Do?*
was first published in 1999 by Clarion Books. Clarion Books is an imprint of
Houghton Mifflin Harcourt Publishing Company.

Houghton Mifflin Books for Children is an imprint of
Houghton Mifflin Harcourt Publishing Company.

www.hmhbooks.com

The text of this book is set in Palatino.
The illustrations for this book were executed in ink and watercolor.

Photograph of brushes on cover and page i © 2013 Houghton Mifflin Harcourt
Photograph of gouache tubes on cover and page i © 2013 Houghton Mifflin Harcourt
Photograph of pen and ink on cover © 2013 Houghton Mifflin Harcourt
Photograph of keyboard on cover © 2013 S.E.A. Photo/Alamy
Photograph of pencils on cover © 2013 Victoria Smith/Houghton Mifflin Harcourt
Photograph of yellow memo on cover © 2013 Christopher Weihs/Alamy
Photograph of wood grain texture on cover © 2013 Randall Fung/Corbis

ISBN 978-0-547-972602

What Do Authors Do? Library of Congress Catalog Control Number 94-19725
What Do Illustrators Do? Library of Congress Catalog Control Number 98-8297

Manufactured in China
SCP 10 9 8 7 6 5 4 3 2 1
4500405483

Part 1
What Do Authors Do?

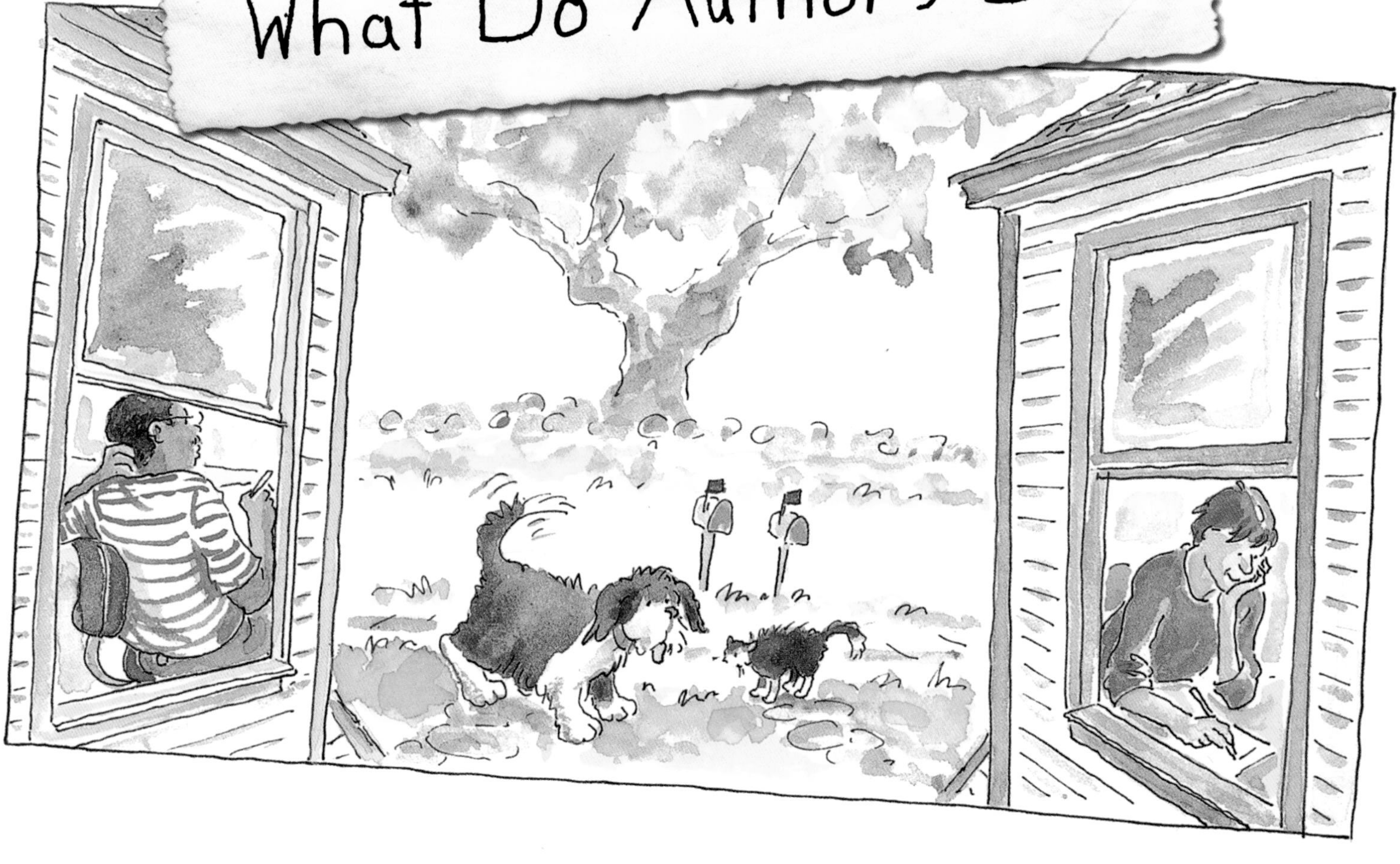

Authors get ideas for books at the strangest moments!

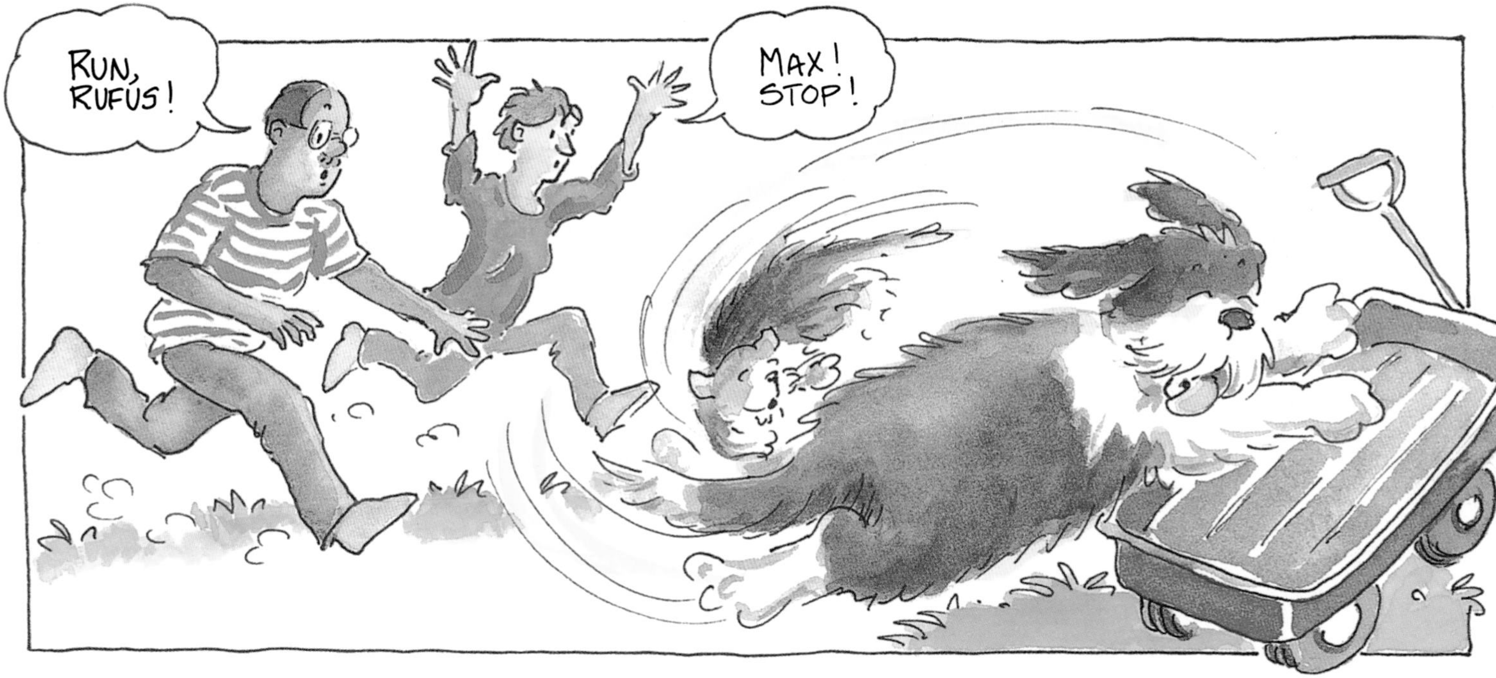
RUN, RUFUS!
MAX! STOP!

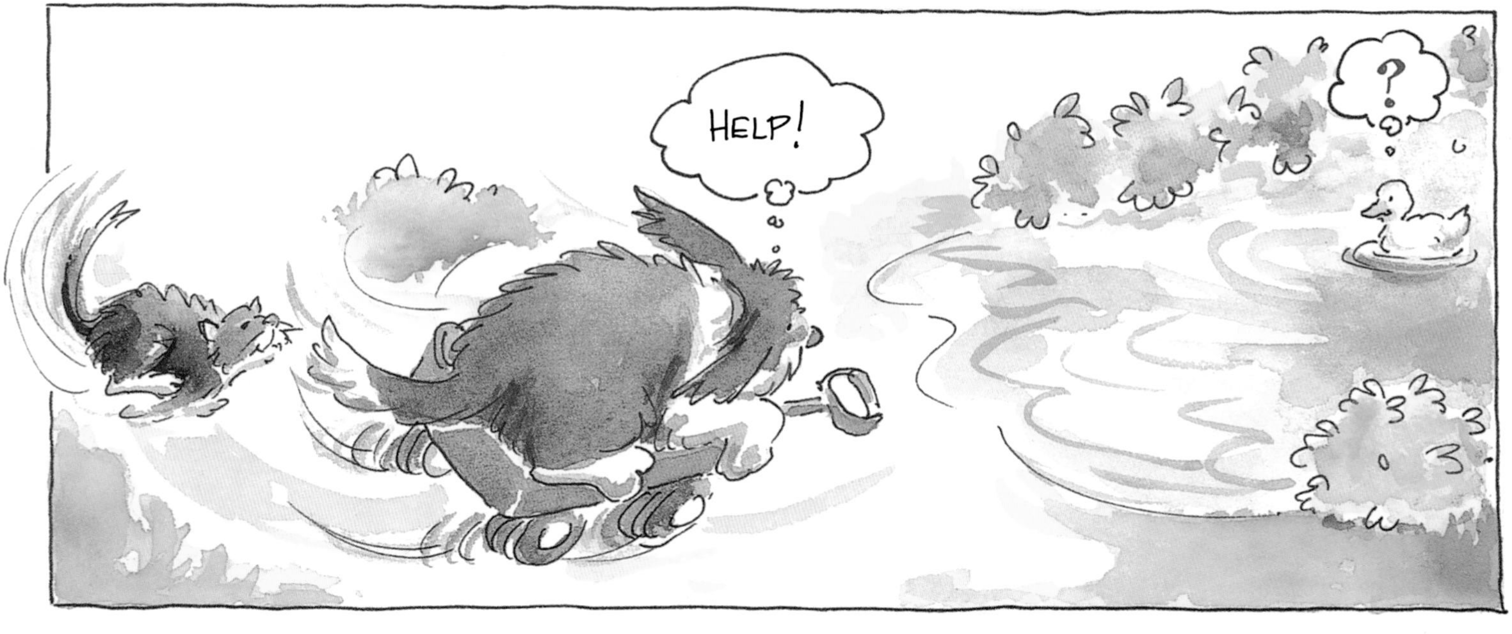
HELP!
?

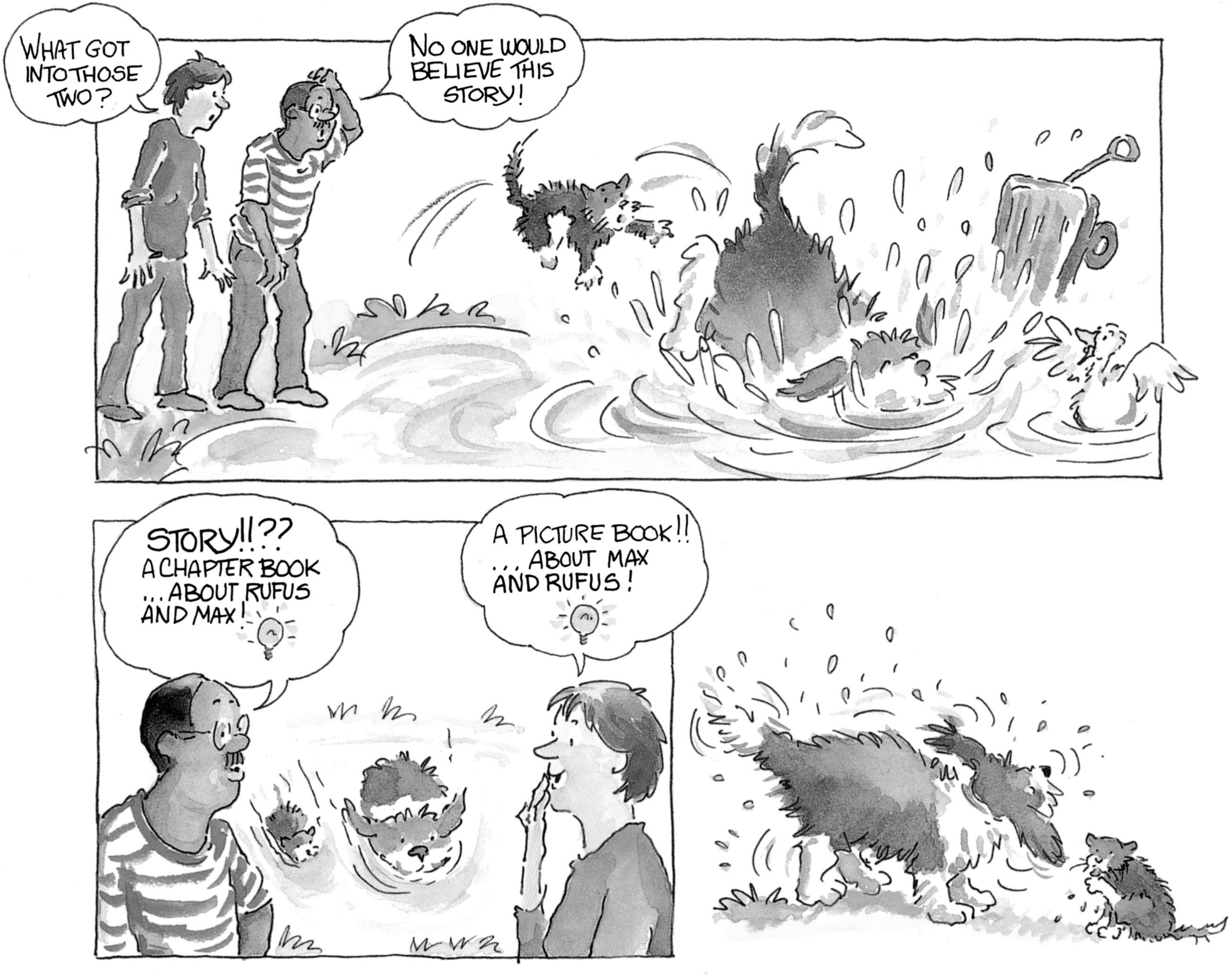
WHAT GOT INTO THOSE TWO?
NO ONE WOULD BELIEVE THIS STORY!
STORY!!??
A CHAPTER BOOK ... ABOUT RUFUS AND MAX!
A PICTURE BOOK!! ... ABOUT MAX AND RUFUS!

When authors have ideas for books, they start to write.

Sometimes it is difficult to find the words.

Some authors write notes about what might happen in the story.
They make lists or outlines.

Some authors who write picture books are also illustrators.
Sometimes they sketch as they write. The sketches give them ideas.

Sometimes authors need more information.

So they go to libraries, historical societies, museums . . .

They read books, old newspapers, magazines, letters, and diaries written long ago. They take notes.

They interview people. They take more notes.

They listen and watch.

They write and write and write . . .

and cross things out . . .

throw parts of the story away . . . and start again.

Sometimes authors read their stories to their families.
Their families make suggestions.

Sometimes they read to author friends in a writers' group.
The friends make suggestions.

Sometimes authors get stuck, so they put their books away for a while.

But usually, when they are doing something else, they get unstuck.

Then they start to write again.

Authors who are also illustrators make a dummy
of the book to show how it will look with illustrations.

It can take one year, two years, or more to finish writing a manuscript!
When the stories are finished, authors send their manuscripts to publishers.

Sometimes they wait for weeks or months to hear whether the publishers
like their books.

Most authors have received rejection letters.
Some rejection letters are encouraging. Some are not.

But authors are very persistent people. They work on their manuscripts
some more. They send their manuscripts out to other publishers.

Authors are very pleased when they find a publisher!

But that is not the end of writing a book. There is still more work to do. Authors have to sign contracts (agreements) with their publishers.

Authors go to the publishers' offices to talk to their editors.

Authors work on their stories with the editors.

Editors suggest ways to make the stories better.

The authors make changes.

After the authors have made all the changes, designers decide how the book will look. They choose the size and the shape of the book. They decide which type styles to use. They design the cover.

Designers, working with editors, choose illustrators for the books.

Picture-book authors who do their own illustrations go over their artwork with the designer. The designer makes suggestions.

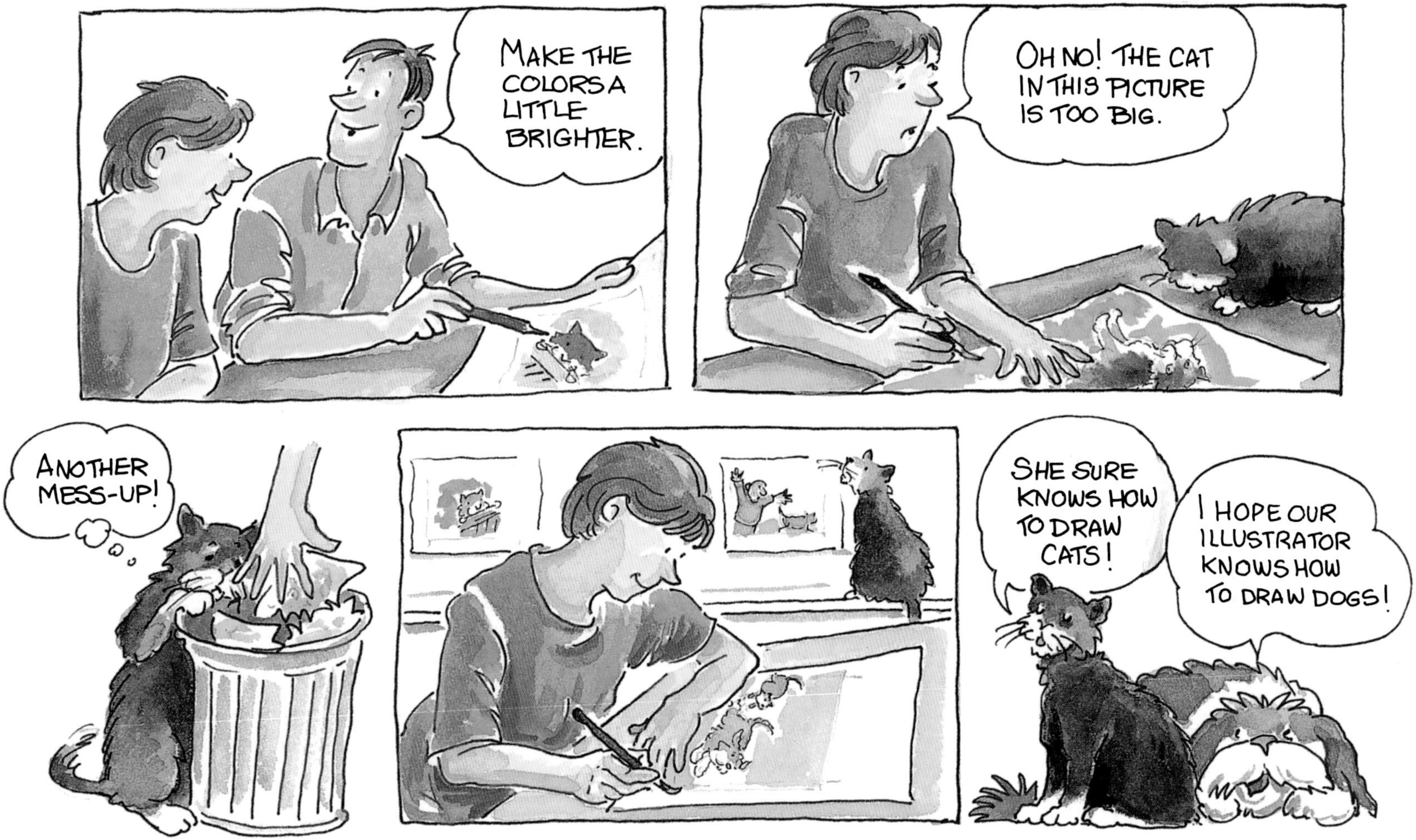

MAKE THE COLORS A LITTLE BRIGHTER.
OH NO! THE CAT IN THIS PICTURE IS TOO BIG.
ANOTHER MESS-UP!
SHE SURE KNOWS HOW TO DRAW CATS!
I HOPE OUR ILLUSTRATOR KNOWS HOW TO DRAW DOGS!

It can take four months or more to finish all of the illustrations for a picture book.

When the illustrations are finished, they need to be checked to see if anything has been left out.

When the story is set in type, it needs to be checked for mistakes.

Don't forget the dedication . . .

. . . or the author photo!

After the authors have sent all the corrections and changes to the publisher, they won't see their books again until they are printed and bound.

When the designers have finished laying out the words and the pictures on the right pages, the authors' books are sent to printers.

THE PRINTED SHEET COMES OUT HERE.

BIG SHEETS OF PAPER GO IN HERE.

THE BOOKS ARE PRINTED ON HUGE PRINTING PRESSES.

MOST OF THE TIME, ALL THE PAGES OF A PICTURE BOOK ARE PRINTED ON ONE BIG SHEET OF PAPER.

THOUSANDS OF COPIES ARE PRINTED IN A FEW HOURS.

A FOLDING MACHINE FOLDS THE PRINTED SHEETS INTO BOOKLETS (SIGNATURES.)

THE OUTER ENDPAPER IS GLUED ONTO THE COVER.

CAT

FOLDED SIGNATURES COME OUT HERE.

TWO SIGNATURES

THE SIGNATURES ARE GATHERED AND STITCHED TOGETHER WITH ENDPAPERS BY OTHER MACHINES.

THE PAGES ARE GLUED INTO THE COVER BY A CASING-IN MACHINE.

The printed sheets of paper go to the bindery, where they are folded, gathered, trimmed, stitched, and glued into covers by huge machines.

The books are finished! Thousands of them! They are packed into boxes and sent to the publishers' warehouses.

Copies are sent to the authors.

Now that the books are published, it's a good time to celebrate.

But the authors start to worry. How are people going to find out about their books? Are people going to like them?

Magazines and newspapers review their books.
Some reviews are wonderful! Some are not.

Authors tell people about their books at schools and libraries.
They answer questions.

They autograph their books at bookstores.

But more important, authors are thinking about ideas for their next books!

Part 2
What Do Illustrators Do?

What do illustrators do?
They tell stories with pictures.

This picture shows where two illustrators live and work.

Suppose those two illustrators each
decided to illustrate *Jack and the Beanstalk.*
Would they tell the story the same way?
Would they draw the same kind of pictures?

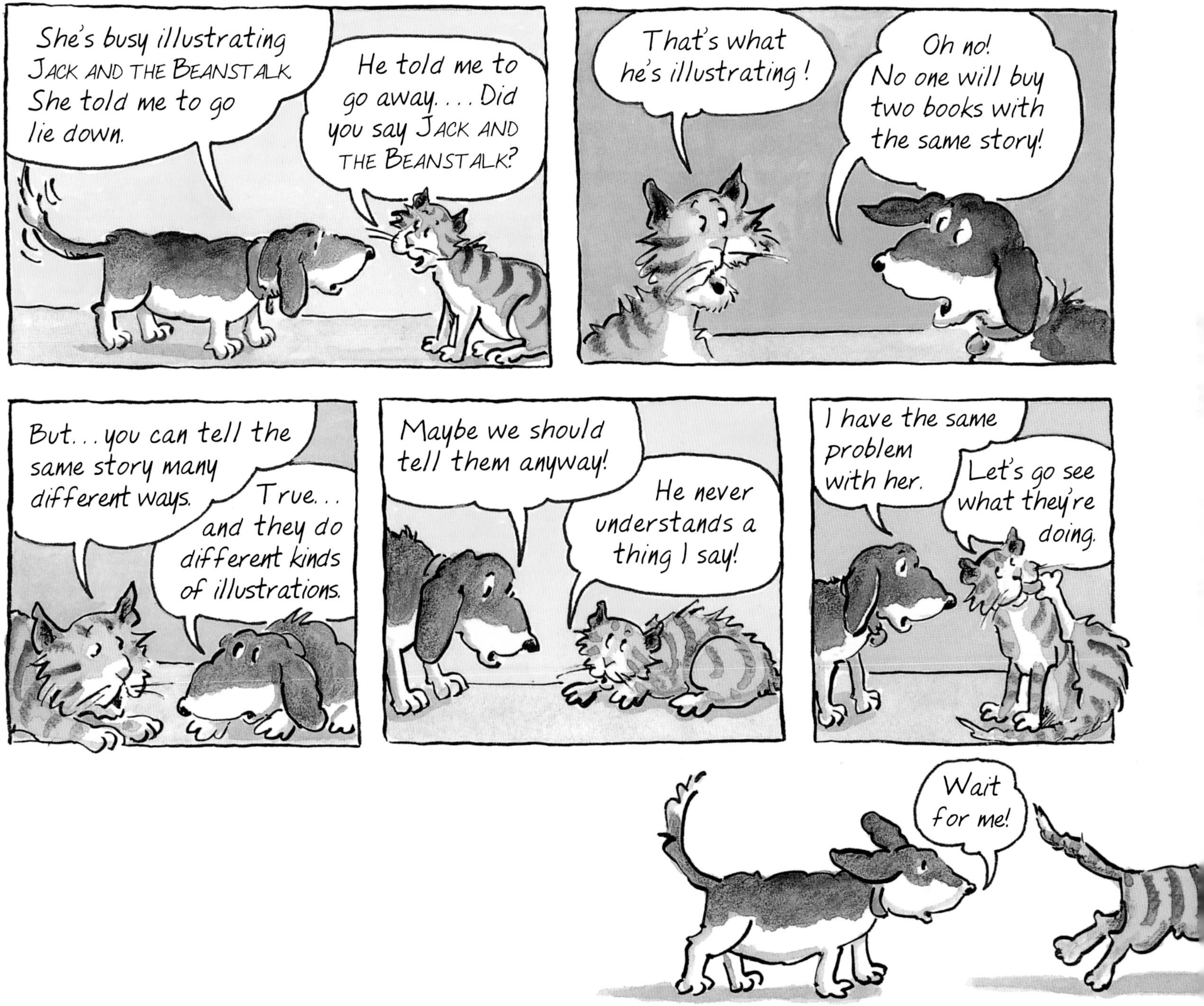
She's busy illustrating JACK AND THE BEANSTALK. She told me to go lie down.
He told me to go away. . . . Did you say JACK AND THE BEANSTALK?
That's what he's illustrating!
Oh no! No one will buy two books with the same story!
But. . . you can tell the same story many different ways.
True. . . and they do different kinds of illustrations.
Maybe we should tell them anyway!
He never understands a thing I say!
I have the same problem with her.
Let's go see what they're doing.
Wait for me!

First, illustrators decide which scenes
in the story they want to illustrate . . .

A plan shows which pictures go on which pages.

The Story of JACK and the BEANSTALK

It's about a boy who plants a magic bean.

The bean sprouts and it grows and GROWS right through the clouds!

Jack climbs to the top of the beanstalk.

What's up there?

A mean, wicked GIANT!

YIKES!

Don't worry! Jack hides. Then, when the giant is asleep, Jack steals the hen that lays golden eggs.

He steals?

The hen wants to be stolen! She hates living with the giant!

So Jack rescues the hen . . . .

Does he become rich and live happily ever after?

He does, but then he climbs the beanstalk two more times.

He takes a sack of gold coins and then a singing harp while the giant is asleep.

But the harp sings and the giant wakes up! He chases Jack . . . .

Jack slides down the beanstalk and the giant is about to slide down too! But...

...Jack chops down the beanstalk!

CRASH!

What happens to the giant?

There are different theories.

Where are you going?

To see how she's doing with her story.

After illustrators make a plan for their book, they need to make a **dummy.** (A dummy is a model of the book.) First they decide what shape and size the book will be.

What is the best shape for a book about a tall, tall, TALL beanstalk? Maybe a vertical rectangle.

I can draw tall beanstalks on single pages...

...or I can draw horizontal pictures across two pages.

Then they make **sketches** of the pictures that will go on each page of the dummy.

The first sketches are often rough scribbles on tracing paper.

This is how we look when we are rough sketches.

This is Jack climbing the beanstalk. What does Jack look like? Where does he live? What do beanstalks look like?

His book is vertical too.

As they are sketching, illustrators need to decide how things will look: the characters, their clothes, the setting.

Illustrators can use their imaginations, or they may have to do some research.

Some illustrators are also authors. They can change their story as they work on the sketches.

Each illustration has
a different problem.
For instance: From what
point of view do you draw
the magic bean being planted?

Should I draw
this picture from
a bird's-eye view?
Close up? Far away?
A mouse's-eye view?

The close up,
bird's-eye view
shows the bean
best.

The mouse
can't see the
bean at all.

How do you draw a beanstalk
so it looks like it's growing?

There is usually more than one way to solve the same problem.

Wow, Mom! The beanstalk must be enormous. Look at the roots!

Those roots are huge compared to Jacqueline!

That night, on the roof directly over Jacqueline's bedroom, the magic bean started to grow. It grew and grew and grew......

Here is another problem:
How do you make a beanstalk
look really TALL?

I could draw Jacqueline looking down the beanstalk...

...or looking up at it.

Things look so small when they are far away. Wait for me!

And things look bigger when they are close up.... That's called perspective.

Illustrators need to think
about the design of each page.

Help! I'm
stuck in
the gutter!

Don't forget to
leave room for
the words!

Don't put important
characters in the
gutter of the book!

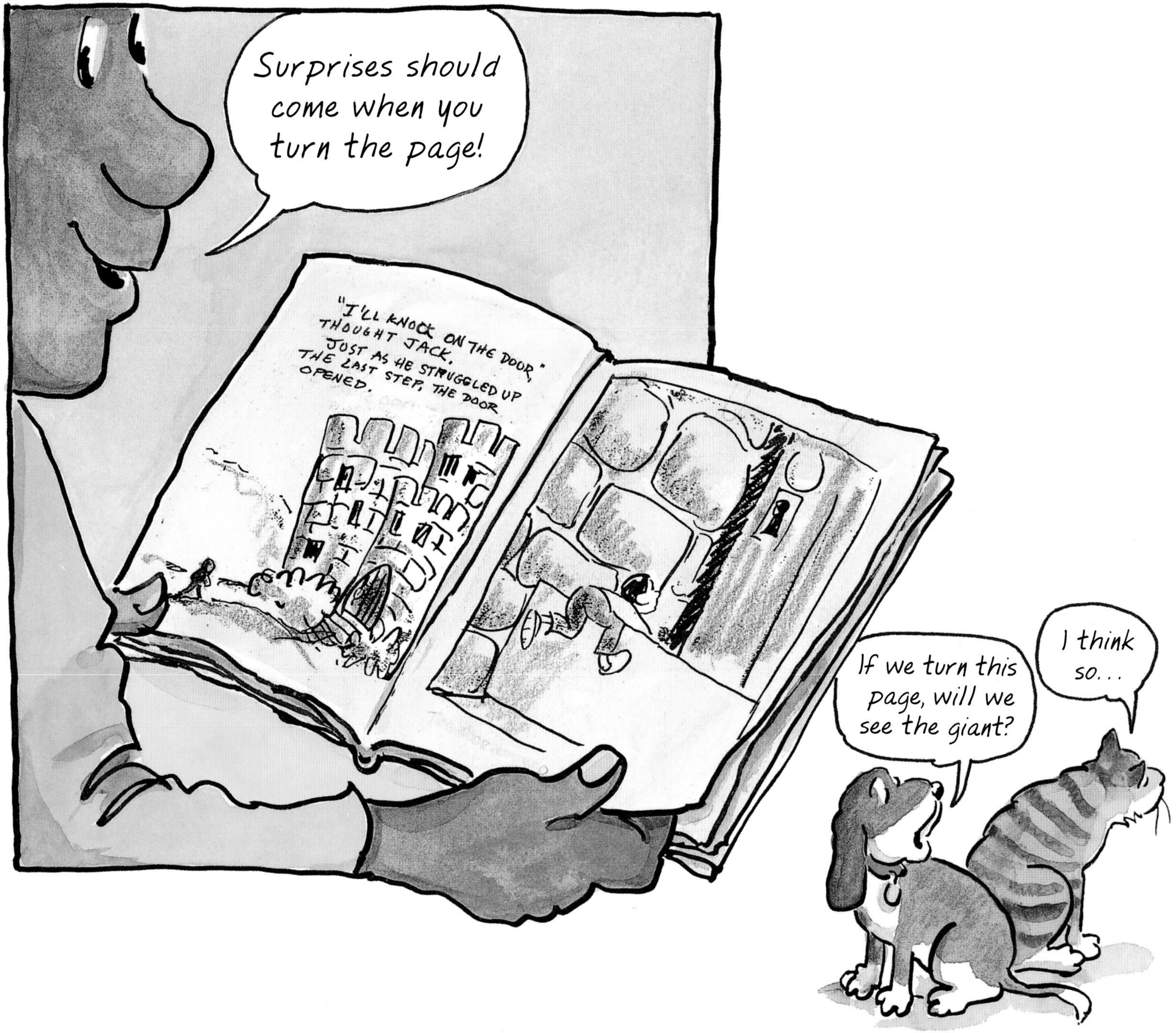
Surprises should come when you turn the page!
"I'LL KNOCK ON THE DOOR," THOUGHT JACK. JUST AS HE STRUGGLED UP THE LAST STEP, THE DOOR OPENED.
If we turn this page, will we see the giant?
I think so. . .

Oops! If the giant doesn't look BIG enough or SCARY enough, the illustrator will draw that picture again.

...and what would Jack see when he looks up at the giant?

These pictures are scarier! And we can only see part of the giant.

Which picture do you think he should use in the book?

How would it feel
to run across a table
right under the nose
of a sleeping GIANT?

Illustrators need to draw
how their characters feel.
(Sometimes they make
faces in a mirror to see how
an expression would look.)

Sometimes illustrators need someone else to model for them.

What are you working on?

My own version of JACK AND THE BEANSTALK

Uh oh!

So am I!

Oh no!

Oh good! Your dummy is different from mine. Different place, different people...

And remember, our illustration styles are very different.

I like both books!

What is style?

It's how they draw the illustrations.

Each illustrator has a different **style** of drawing, just as every person has a different style of handwriting.

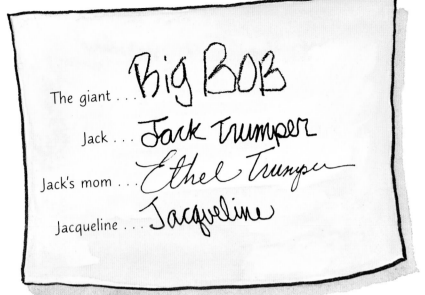

The giant . . . Big BOB

Jack . . . Jack Trumper

Jack's mom . . . Ethel Trumper

Jacqueline . . . Jacqueline

Different styles for drawing Jack and Jacqueline

We're trying a new style.

When illustrators have finished their dummies, they show them to the editor and the designer at the publishing company.

The editor decides whether the pictures tell the story.

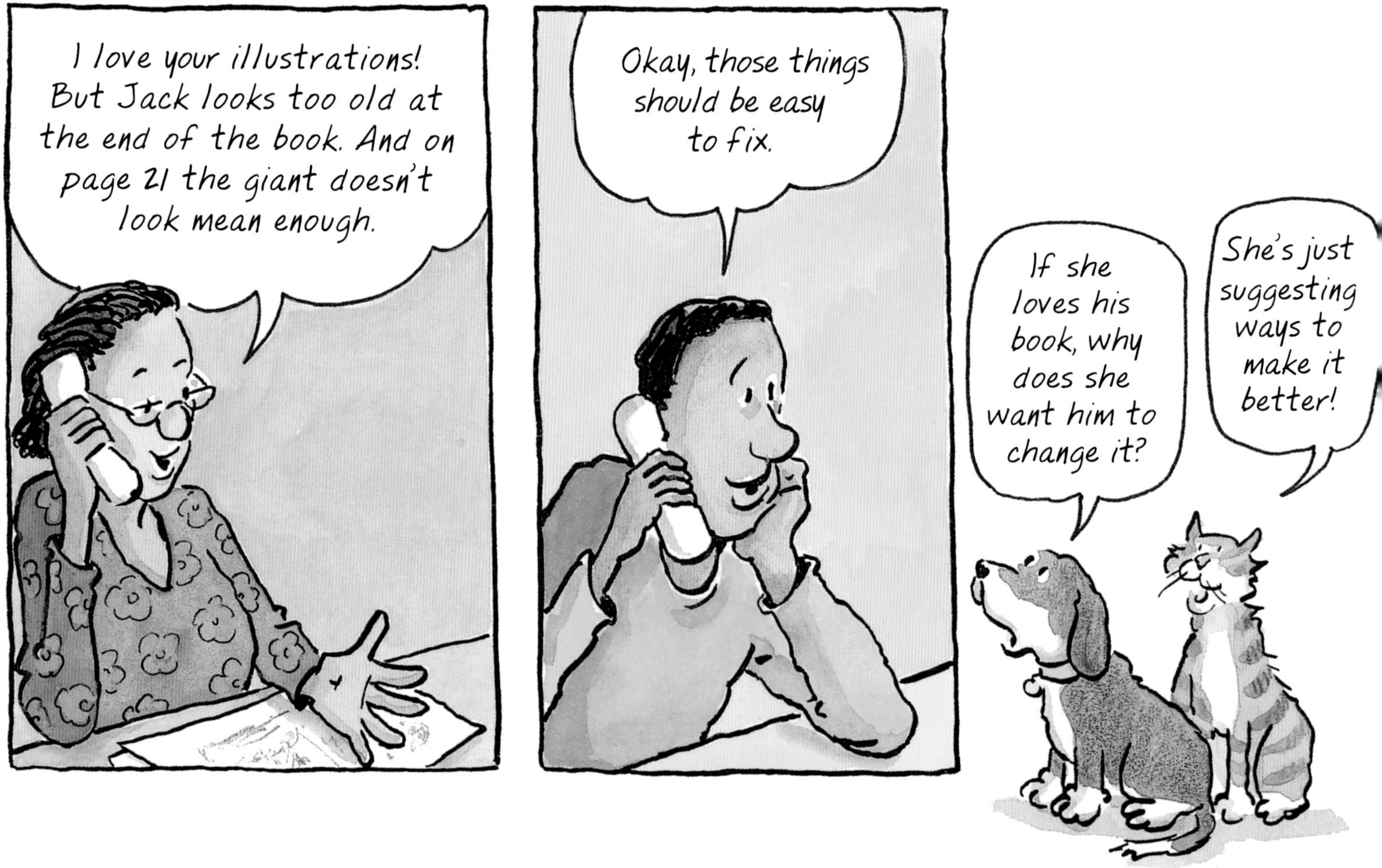
I love your illustrations! But Jack looks too old at the end of the book. And on page 21 the giant doesn't look mean enough.
Okay, those things should be easy to fix.
If she loves his book, why does she want him to change it?
She's just suggesting ways to make it better!

The designer makes suggestions about the design of the book.

She chooses the typeface for the words and the cover.

I think the book could be a little bigger.

I'd love that!

I'm sending you the type. I hope you like it.

Sample typefaces for title:

Jack and the Beanstalk

Jack and the Beanstalk

Jack and the Beanstalk

Sample typefaces for text:

(easy to read)

While Jacqueline slept in her bedroom below, the magic bean grew . . . and grew . . .

(not so easy to read)

While Jacqueline slept in her bedroom below, the magic bean grew . . . and grew . . .

What do you think of this typeface?

I can't read a thing you are saying.

59

Illustrators need to decide how they want to do the finished illustrations.

They can draw different kinds of lines and textures with different kinds of tools.

I'm trying different kinds of lines... pencil, pen, brush.

pencil

brush

pen with flexible point

felt tip pen

Look! I can paint!

They can color their
illustrations with paint,
pastels, pencils, or crayons . . .

I'm experimenting.
I've tried watercolors,
watercolor crayons,
and colored pencils.

watercolors

watercolor crayons

colored pencils

They can do an illustration without any black line at all!

Illustrators go to art stores to buy their supplies.

They need to choose the paper they want to use for their finished illustrations.

Some papers are good for water-color, others for pastel, others for pencil . . .

Some are smooth. Some are textured.

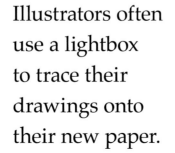

Illustrators often use a lightbox to trace their drawings onto their new paper.

63

Sometimes illustrators
throw away their pictures
and start again.

Sometimes they change the colors.

Too many cool colors! Blue flowers, blue shoes, green leaves.

Cool colors make you feel cool, calm, relaxed or sometimes sad.

I need to add some warm colors - reds, oranges, yellows.

Well, maybe not that many!

Warm colors make you feel bright, wild, loud, red hot!

Or they may change
the composition.

It can take months to finish all the illustrations for a picture book.

Before they are sent to the publisher, they need to be checked to make sure nothing is left out.

Illustrators often do the cover of the book last. The cover tells a lot about a story: What is it about? Does it look interesting?

Would these covers make you want to read the books?

This illustration tells how the two illustrators celebrated when they finally finished all that work!

P.S.—From the (Real) Author-Illustrator

When we were looking over the proofs for this two-book collection, we decided we needed to talk about a NEW tool that some illustrators are now using...

Tell them how you use the computer for drawing and painting!

The computer for drawing and painting? **WHY?**

Remember when I drew that pen and ink picture of you and it was too small?

—YUP!

So...I had to draw **another** LARGER picture...

The larger picture was goofy!

Yeah, so she drew it again and again!

Wireless, pressure sensitive pen

But NOW, she draws with a special pen on an electronic tablet hooked into the computer!

Electronic tablet

She can make you larger without redrawing!

She can move us, color us...

...with different textures: chalk, watercolor

She can change you in all kinds of ways!

Hey look! She redrew me after all!

Some illustrators use the computer ONLY for drawing or ONLY for coloring. And some use it for both.

And many still prefer real pencils, pens and brushes!

Did she illustrate these two pages on that tablet?

Yep!

71

Photograph © Jeff Baird

Eileen Christelow has written and illustrated many fun and funny picture books, including the popular Five Little Monkeys series, *Vote!*, and *Letters from a Desperate Dog*. She and her husband, Ahren, live in Vermont.

For more information about the Five Little Monkeys, fun activities, information on how illustrations are created, and comic strips, visit **WWW.CHRISTELOW.COM** and **WWW.FIVELITTLEMONKEYS.COM.**

Budding Writer & Illustrator Activities

What you will need:

1. A notebook or drawing pad

2. A pen or pencil

3. Your imagination!

Getting an Idea

The authors you met talked about finding ideas for stories in the strangest places. Sometimes you do not need to think too much about an idea. It may just pop into your head when you are walking to school, eating ice cream, taking a shower, or riding in the car.

Brainstorming is quickly writing down all of the ideas that pop into your head. You don't have

to worry about them, just get all of the ideas out. Next, look at them again.

One of the easiest ways to get an idea, or start to brainstorm, is by asking questions, especially "What if" questions.

You can start by asking questions about the world, people, and animals around you. For example, what if your cat could talk? What if all the rubber bands in the world disappeared? What if you woke up tomorrow and you were invisible?

Think of some "What if" questions. Do you think that one could start an idea for a story? Get a notebook and start writing those brilliant ideas down!

Finding the Right Word

One of the best parts about writing a story is coming up with the right word to say exactly what you want to say. Some words sound silly, some sound scary, some make you feel happy. Usually there is more than one word that will work.

Think about how different words sound and what you think of when you hear

them. What does the word "ooze" make you think of? Maybe it makes you think of slime or frogs (or slimy frogs!). Look at the words below.
What do these words make you think of?

gooey • **fang** • **glitter** • **giant** • **beast**
kitty • **cat** • **castle** • **kooky** • **fuzzy**

Write down some of your favorite words in your notebook. You can look back at this list when you start writing your story.

Telling and Retelling

The illustrators in this book tell the same basic story two different ways. Though the story is *Jack and the Beanstalk*, each illustrator added their own style, made changes, and came out with a unique, or one-of-a kind, story. One illustrator made Jack into Jacqueline; the other had Jack's cat watch the beanstalk grow.

Pick a fairy tale like *Jack and the Beanstalk* or a folk tale like *Chicken Little* and see how you can tell it differently from the version you know. What would you keep the same? What would you change? How could you put a different spin on the story?

You know what to do—write down those ideas!

Creating the Characters

Choose a couple of characters from one of your story ideas. What do they look like? What are they wearing? What details tell us about who they are? Think about what items they may carry or have around them. For example, if your character is a painter, he or she might have paint on their clothes; if your character is a writer, he or she might carry a pen.

Sketch your character and write down some details about his or her personality.

Point of View

When you are an illustrator, you get to decide what point of view you are using to draw your picture, or how you are looking at what you are drawing. There are many different points of view.

You can look at a scene straight on. Is it close up or far away?

You can use a bird's-eye view, which is looking down at a scene from above.

Or you could look from a mouse's-eye view, which is looking up at a scene from below.

You can draw from the point of view of a character, drawing only what you imagine your character would see.

Part of your point of view is deciding how much or how little you want to show in your picture. Do you want to show all of the scene or just focus on a part of it?

Look at the two covers that the artists made for their Jack and the Beanstalk stories. What points of view do you notice? What do they tell you about the story?

For example, how does it make you feel to see just the giant's massive feet coming toward Jack? Would it be scarier if you saw all of the giant? What if Jack was looking up at the giant's face? What if the giant was looking down at Jack?

Now practice drawing a landscape in your sketchpad. It could be the opening scene of your fairy tale retelling. Rough out the features of your landscape. Is it a scary beginning, or a peaceful one? Which features, like a craggy mountain or a winding river, make it that way? How much of the landscape is in your picture? Will you show as much of the landscape as you can, or will you focus on one part of it?

Now try putting a character in it. Will your character be very small in it, as if you are seeing him or her from far away, or close up? Will you show him or her from the front, back, or side?

Making the Cover

Think about one of your story ideas. Think about the characters. What do you want people to know about your story? What do you think would make people interested in reading it? What do you want your cover to look like?

Design your cover, or just jot down ideas and pictures that you might want to use.

By now, after completing just these few little exercises, you should be well on your way toward writing and illustrating your own original story or fairy tale!